POPULAR
LONGING

ALSO BY NATALIE SHAPERO

Hard Child
No Object

NATALIE SHAPERO

POPULAR LONGING

COPPER CANYON PRESS

PORT TOWNSEND, WASHINGTON

Cover art: Jamie Boyle, *Ventriloquist Dummy's Shirt,* 2007–2017. Cigarette smoke-stained
cotton shirt, black and red cotton thread, 20 × 16–18 × 2 inches.

Copper Canyon Press is in residence at Fort Worden State Park in Port Townsend,
Washington, under the auspices of Centrum. Centrum is a gathering place for artists
and creative thinkers from around the world, students of all ages and backgrounds, and
audiences seeking extraordinary cultural enrichment.

LIBRARY OF CONGRESS CATALOGING-IN-PUBLICATION DATA
Names: Shapero, Natalie, author.
Title: Popular longing / Natalie Shapero.
Description: Port Townsend, Washington : Copper Canyon Press, [2020] |
Summary: "A collection of poems by Natalie Shapero"—Provided by publisher.
Identifiers: LCCN 2020030263 | ISBN 9781556595882 (paperback)
Subjects: LCGFT: Poetry.
Classification: LCC PS3619.H35575 P67 2020 | DDC 811/.6—dc23
LC record available at https://lccn.loc.gov/2020030263

COPPER CANYON PRESS
Post Office Box 271
Port Townsend, Washington 98368
www.coppercanyonpress.org

for Meg Shevenock

CONTENTS

3   Man at His Bath

7   My Hair Is My Thing

8   The Suggested Face for Sorry

9   Lying Is Getting

10   Five by Seven

11   California

13   A Space to Train and Exit

14   Magpie

15   Tea

16   Have at It

17   Tomatoes Ten Ways

18   They Said It Couldn't Be Done

19   It for Me

20   Sunshower

21   Green

22   Totally under the Water

23   Long Wedding

25   The Greatest Two Minutes in Sports

26   You Missed a Spot

27   Weekend

28   Stoop

29   Flowers Would Have Killed You

30   The Lone Acceptable Application of Daylight

31   Say It to My Face

32   Good Share

34   It Used to Be We Had to Go to War

35   During the Strife, My Sisters

36   And Also with You

37   Good Description

38   The Beach

41   Don't Spend It All in One Place

57   Other Things, If Not More Urgent Things

58   Some Toxin

59   Fake Sick

60   Home, Followed by Tall Buildings

61   And Stay Out

62   Ohio on TV

64   Fifty

65   Pennsylvania

67   *Acknowledgments*

69   *About the Author*

POPULAR
LONGING

Man at His Bath

Six years ago, the big museum sold eight famous paintings
to purchase, for unspecified millions,
Gustave Caillebotte's MAN AT HIS BATH.
Now it's hip to have a print of it,
and whenever I see one hung for decoration,
I'm almost certain that this is what Caillebotte
had in mind when he broke out the oils
in 1884: some twenty-first-century bitch in Boston
catching a glimpse of a framed reproduction,
recollecting a study about how washing oneself may induce
a sense of culpability. What I remember

is he insisted I clean before leaving. That, and he was
trying to be dreamlike. He took my jaw in his hand
and said IN THE NEXT LIFE, WE'LL REALLY BE TOGETHER,
and the clamp in his voice made me almost
certain he knew something I did not. Now I eat right,
train hard, get my shots. This life—I'm angling
to remain in this life as long as I can, being almost
certain, as I am, what's after—

I do not like money, neither for itself nor for what it can buy, as I want nothing we know about.

René Magritte

My Hair Is My Thing

The symphony's out of funding again, and no
wonder: all those violins, the twisted strands
and sponges—who could not think
of torture? Last week I read a novel about a man
so awful that when he died I wept
because it was fiction. I wanted it to be real
so I could watch him really die.
I wanted you to die also, and to be feted
with a lengthy, organza-filled funeral,
so that I could make a big show
of blowing it off. I decided to go out
and get a tattoo of your funeral with me not there,
but apparently it's illegal here to tattoo
a person who's crying. The trend now
is to be interred with beloved possessions:
pearl-trimmed gun, gold watch,
whatever you've got. Some people recoil
at the waste of it, but not me. These contused little
objects of wealth—they're disgusting. I just
pray we have earth and shovels enough. I pray
we have bodies enough to bury them all.

The Suggested Face for Sorry

You and me—we are the opposite
of twins in an old story.
When I am in pain, you don't feel it.
If I up and retch, you never guess.

The city laid out poison
along the tunnels and tracks, meant
for rats, and one day my dog ate some.
She was fine. I've never been
so jealous in my life. I want to do
the things we do to die,
and then just take off sprinting
in the steep ravine. In my dream,

I walk my dog and you cross
our path and she torques at you
and rears and snaps. She senses
you are wholly bad. They say animals

can tell, like with earthquakes.
You're supposed to scan the classifieds,
searching for a sudden spike
in the number of missing pets. That's
how you know to prepare. Maneuver
away from shelving. Crawl
to the nearest doorframe. Get out
of California. What are you waiting for.

Lying Is Getting

to me. The high-ups instructed me not to tell their dad
about the particulates—the last
time he caught them polluting, he made them sit
themselves down right there and eat a whole smokestack.
I keep nodding when the city insists I stick
with the story of accidents—she was cleaning
her gun, he was cleaning the recessed
sign on the front of the passenger train, they were holding
hands and had a whole plan to clean
the concrete twenty-two stories below the ledge
of the mixed-use downtown
tower. To really make it shine. The party line
is getting me good. I keep turning
my face to the flashbulb in an effort to seem like someone
with no secrets, and now when I see other people
framed and beaming, I want to know what they're keeping
in. All those holiday moments, tacked
to the fridge or strung up with wire and eyelets. All that sin—

Five by Seven

Really, when people have photographs of themselves
displayed on their walls, I just assume
they have died and it is their ghosts
who've invited me over, their ghosts with whom
I'm sharing a meal, making small
talk about all the bodies and trash on Mount Everest.
Oh lacquered ghosts, so high on your own
finished triptych of fetes
and feats and the corresponding assurance
you go unforgotten—let's

go out. From the recent restaurant
boom, infer a citywide uptick in rage-ravaged homes.
People want new spots to fight, to squall
and snipe, lose their appetites, be brought
the chalkboard special, not touch it,
see it whisked to the kitchen and scraped
out back for a dog to eat, but that's cool—dogs
have to eat, too—

California

We often ate late by flameless
candles and took turns choosing
how best to be disposed of.
I want to be buried. I want everyone
to be buried. I realize there's scarcely
a spare acre left in the ground, but I just
can't do without the indecorous
transit from parlor to plot.
I need the array of daytime headlights
jolting the arid access road,
the only remembrance that matters.
Don't make a speech.

For years I would wonder whether
the man who attacked me—
in his memory, did the event of it
persist as a dull sort of flash? Then
he died and became himself
just a flash in the mind of the world.
Now I wonder—is he anywhere?
I don't believe in Hell and also I don't
believe in nothing, so that leaves only
Heaven. I have a couple
questions. It is my understanding
that the weather in Heaven

has only a single setting,
which is PLEASANT. I haven't
spent real time in California, but friends
of mine who've moved there
say it's challenging, absent the changing
of the seasons, to remember when things
took place. With reference to always

the lodgepole pine and the low-bent
needlegrass, you get confused.
Dates and sequences, even the people
involved. You can almost imagine
the whole thing was somebody else.

A Space to Train and Exit

Maybe California's just plain easier,
with the commonness
of outbuildings. Raw-looking cedar or sheet
metal walls and a runnel
of sun getting in through the roof seams.
Position the heavy bag, tighten the eyebolt,
twenty-five right hooks. Or pull up
a chair and compose your suicide note.
A space to train and exit.

The purpose of having a body at all
is to practice, to practice
the keeping alive of domestic
animals and plants. You dispense to yourself
some minerals and water. You expose
yourself to the sun and it helps
you remember to do the same for those
in your charge. If you could equip
them with all they require, or make them

require nothing, you wouldn't
need your body at all.

Magpie

Unusual rain of late, and a new weed
that resembles concertina wire
is threading itself through the dirt.

Seeing it makes me think of never seeing it again,

how I will miss this upstart greenness
after I lose it all and am thrown
from this home, which will be soon.

It'll be someone else living here then, hiding

an emergency key in a bucket,
up late snaking the bath drain or early
doing sit-ups on the painted floor.

It'll be someone else walking a mile and a half

to the store called Magpie, buying
a gift for whichever friend's baby, rattle
or small shirt with a transit map.

The name is meant to conjure up a gorgeous, inky

creature culling treasures to bring
back, but if you really get close
to a magpie's nest, you see it's all trash.

Tea

I can't get away from it.
Felted-up reenactors shoving a great fake crate of it
into the Harbor and jeering.
After the tour group leaves, they fish it
back out and towel it off,
unbutton their waistcoats to smoke.
At the nearby counter-service place, there are two
jars next to the register, and dropping bills
into one or the other is how
we affirm our commitments—why should we ever
pay decently, unless it occurs
in this fever of rivalry that passes for fun?
What are our choices and might I suggest
LESS IS MORE against MORE IS MORE?
Or IT COULD HAPPEN ANYTIME against IT HAPPENS
ALL THE TIME? Or how about THIS VIOLENCE
FOREVER UNDOES A PERSON
against THAT CONTENTION CAN ONLY
BE ROOTED IN THE RETROGRADE
VIEW THAT A WOMAN IS EITHER INTACT OR SHE'S
NOT? I always thought I'd made
peace with THIS PLANET, and yet here I am
shoving all my cash in the jar
marked ANYPLACE ELSE. There isn't enough
money in the world.

Have at It

When you work here for ten years, you get
a blanket. The blanket has their name on it,
not yours. I am conducting an anecdotal
survey of longtime employees, and I have yet
to find one person who uses the thing
to keep warm. M reported placing it
between her children and the dirt
before they all sat down to a meal outside.
S recounted how she'd wrestled it out
of a half-stuck bureau drawer to wrap
her beagle's body after he died.
She'd buried the dog herself, in her bloomless
little side yard, and registered
embarrassment when the meter reader
caught her there, intoning over the body
with a hymnal. But why should she be
embarrassed? It certainly can't be beneath us
to bless our animal dead, when all
our scientists do all day is endeavor to prove
that great apes mourn, that elephants
mourn, that houseflies mourn, that when
a fiddle-leaf ficus succumbs, another ficus
keens in its earthenware. We would like to
confirm that everyone is recognized in death.
Unseen as we are in this life, it's all we have.

Tomatoes Ten Ways

On a lampless arc of interstate, playing
I DON'T SPY, the nighttime game

where you say what you don't see and wait
for someone else to also fail to see it—

are we there yet? I just want to get

back now, back to my kitchen, back
to my peeler and ladle and electric
oven where decades of hands

have worn the temperature marks
clean off the dial—it's always a guess.

Cooking is important. It prepares us

for how to sustain each other
in the emptiness ahead. A bread
for sharing, braided with strips

of garbage. A novel kind of starchy pie

baked over one tea light. Children,
today was sent here by the future

to beg you to think of this place
like a body—it might be yours

for now, but it is only a matter of time
before it buckles and kicks and ousts
you and sinks, like the very

body it is, right back to the ground.

They Said It Couldn't Be Done

So sorry about the war—we just kind of
wanted to learn how to swear
in another language, and everyone knows

the top method is simply to open
fire and listen to what people yell.

And now here's God again with His hand

crank, lowering the sky to make more room
for Himself. And now here's the high-rise

we build to brace back, this series of holes
for bathing and mending and parboiling

roots and undecorated fucking in the style

of the times: one person half-braying,
the other admonishing KEEP IT
DOWN—I DON'T WANT THE WAR TO HEAR.

It for Me

Don't worry. Wars are like children—
you create one, offer scant
effort, then call it botched as the years
accrue, go off and make
a new one with somebody else.
A chance to finally get it right.

People love stories of tyrants
expiring in prison, as though an entire
reign of thrown roses and feasts
on command might be somehow erased
by the precast concrete, the drain
in the center of the floor.

But it's not like anyone gets some ideal
death—handshakes all around
and then snuggling in velvet, saying
THAT'S IT FOR ME! What matters
is what you do with your best
years. No one can take that away.

Sunshower

Some people say the devil is beating
his wife. Some people say the devil
is pawing his wife. Some people say
the devil is doubling down on an overall
attitude of entitlement toward
the body of his wife. Some people
say the devil won't need to be sorry,
as the devil believes that nothing
comes after this life. Some people say
that in spite of the devil's public,
longstanding, and meticulously
logged disdain for the health
and wholeness of his wife, the devil
spends all day, every day, insisting
grandly and gleefully on his general
pro-woman ethos, that the devil truly
considers himself to be an unswayed
crusader: effortlessly magnetic,
scrupulous, gracious, and, in spite of
the devil's several advanced degrees,
a luminous autodidact. Some people
say calm down; this is commonplace.
Some people say calm down;
this is very rare. Some people say
the sun is washing her face. Some
people say in Hell, they're having a fair.

Green

I saw an image of Cleopatra being delivered
to Caesar in a rolled-up rug, just falling
from the rug, and at work I began to be worried
that others, and especially those in supervisory roles,
viewed me as green. Temperamentally inexpert.
I tried wearing crisper shirts, but it didn't help.
So of course when all my friends began
to die, I found at last a means of proving
myself through inattention to their passing.
I refrained from sharing remembrances,
that time we pulled B's ruined tooth
or when L and I hiked out to the obverse
side of the Hollywood sign. When colleagues
sought to console me, I offered only the stoic
rejoinder DEATH IS A PART OF LIFE.
I underwent my yearly performance assessment
and was prompted to name a task at which
I excelled. I responded TRULY KNOWING
THAT DEATH IS A PART OF LIFE, and when
they requested I then articulate a plan
for the coming year, I said SPEAKING LOUDER
WHEN STATING THAT DEATH IS A PART OF LIFE,
AND PERHAPS APPENDING AN AMPLIFYING
GESTURE. I returned to my desk and removed
my heels and capped my pen and called B's mom
and told her about the tooth. She recounted
for me his younger years, mud covered or up to his
shoulders in the cold ocean. She said he had been
ready to die, that through his suffering he'd sworn it
several times. Though also he'd said several
times that he wasn't ready. It was tough to know.

Totally under the Water

He knew, he said, he was dying
when for two straight weeks he dreamed of
trying to switch on a swing-arm
lamp that wouldn't switch on. In baths
I've never gone—as they do in the movies,
to demonstrate crux and contemplation—
totally under the water, but if
I did, I would ponder the woman
flooring it into the cinderblock
wall from fifty feet away. I don't think that image
comes from the movies. I think it comes
from the future. The future, with its color
palette of airport whites and its
unrushed glance, its involute
beckoning. I see it. I can see it. At least
somebody wants me.

Long Wedding

Through it all—the usher's nod, the Pachelbel,
the thousand psalms, the joke misplacing
of the rings—I waited for the pause
to acknowledge the few scattered uncles
and friends too ill to attend. I waited for the silence
and the KEEP THEM IN YOUR THOUGHTS.
And keep them in my thoughts I did—I thought
of them so much that I missed all the dancing, all
the sling-back twirls, the forced displays
of riotousness, the cake. I missed all the children
being instructed not to touch the begonias,
and the paper lanterns almost catching fire.
I missed the plastic chimney glasses, emptied
of their cocktails, being set on a table and swept
down into a bag. I missed the part where they
honeymooned in Lisbon. I missed it
when they bought the house with the mudroom
and the mansard roof. I missed it when they retired
somewhere placid. I missed their birthdays, every
year, and then I missed it when they died
and were buried in the dirt with their jewelry on.
I was still sitting there at the rented table,
in front of a single charred onion on a skewer,
thinking of all the guests who had to decline,
thinking of them in hospitals, attended to by loved
ones who had little to say aside from
I HATE HOSPITALS, but whose tenderness
still carried through. I was thinking of the times
I have attempted to exit my body. I was thinking
of how I'd had nowhere to go. I was wishing
for a smaller body hidden within my body,
a smaller site to which I might retreat.
I was wishing for a canny escape not only

from what is around us, but also from what
is pitiless and ambulant and tacky and can lodge
one layer beneath the surface layer of our very
skin. Only under that is where we are.

The Greatest Two Minutes in Sports

Brims and booze and paneled
rooms and paintings

titled GO MAN GO and PHARAOH

What explains

Have we coevolved with waste
and are we here

to be its forward vessel

How long until science
admits that we are worthless

except as carriers

Instinctively we nurse it, we pass it
down, we're done

You Missed a Spot

In movies, a noblewoman is always pointing
her ecru fingernail at a single

unexceptional floorboard, hissing at the servant
girl YOU MISSED A SPOT.

It's supposed to be a peak humiliation—
the more acute the act of cleaning, the worse.

The more acute the working. The more acute
the ferrying of worth from one colossus to the next.

We're like bees, just trying to eat,
and in the process conscripted into transport.

Did you hear the snowdrops are having a baby.
We don't even know what a baby is.

Weekend

Some people despise doing laundry, but I don't
mind it, and I think we can all agree it feels so good
to engage in something you don't
mind. To have a neutral feeling. My only two childhood
memories are hearing the song EVERYBODY'S WORKING
FOR THE WEEKEND and seeing the bumper
sticker THE LABOR MOVEMENT: THE FOLKS WHO
BROUGHT YOU THE WEEKEND. I gathered
the weekend is the portion of life that is understood
to matter. Now that I'm grown, I know that just means
sex. THE LABOR MOVEMENT: THE FOLKS WHO
BROUGHT YOU SEX. Though of course
there are other things to be enjoyed. I DON'T WANT
TO BE PITIED said my neighbor, after explaining to me
she hated her children—not children in general,
but just her own. Her idea of a weekend
is not being pitied. Is someone else having about her
a neutral feeling. Our neighborhood is overrun
with garbage, and the summer makes it reek,
which ruins the otherwise neutral
feeling I have regarding the sun and the sense
of it on me. It's not that I think of myself as my own
child—it's more that I think of my body
as an animal that, having been bred with abandon,
requires a human steward, like those dogs unable
to birth without assistance, without someone
snapping on gloves and boiling the kettle
and cleaning the cotton sheets like I'm doing now,
clipping them up to dry in the sun. It feels so good.

Stoop

All I can think, when I catch the dog out by the stoop
with a rat in her mouth, is I THOUGHT IT WOULD
NEVER HAPPEN TO ME—

                                 that's what the rat, I say
to myself, must be saying, having surely borne witness
to how many other rats gnawed on by how
many herders and hounds and yet fancying, all
that time, herself immune. And don't get her started

on the thorniest part—how the fact that it happens
so frequently means her misery's nothing
special, how the moment of her truest trauma is also
the pinnacle of her own commonness, and it's juvenile
to cry for the everyday—so get over

                                   yourself, I say
to the rat, who squeaks each time the dog
bites down, sounding just like those rubber chew
toys, which I suddenly understand are made to make
the noise of something getting killed—

Flowers Would Have Killed You

The river is heavy with phosphorus and scum.
It causes liver damage if ingested.
I don't know exactly whose runoff it is, but so long
as they're taking press photos with prizewinning
children and donating sizable
sums to the ballet, I take no issue. River's yours.

Once I saw a guy struggling to talk his way out
of some base thing he'd done, and his underwhelmed
companion said to him FLOWERS
WOULD HAVE KILLED YOU? Now I say it

all the time. The councilman announces he's sorry
for taking advantage of the district's trust,
or the paper issues the mother
of all retractions, and I'm right there at the window,
readying myself for the knock and the spray
of larkspur and tea rose. You shouldn't have.

The Lone Acceptable Application of Daylight

is in the expression PUT A LITTLE
DAYLIGHT between you and what's
troubling, set out moving,
distance yourself from the pharaonic
shade of the household names and the power

couples. The quality of cloud in one locale
or another, solace of the contrail
noon—who cares? Why even
look up, when all we'll see is people
looking down? Their grapefruit juice

on the balcony. Their news. Their delight
at the sight of us. We entertain them.
We kiss and spit and strike. We're always
changing. They like it when
we fight: I'LL KNOCK THE LIVING—

Say It to My Face

In this age of nostalgia, all I really have
is how, speeding by the salt-bitten building
where I used to live, I don't point it out.
What a lowly source of pride—the refusal
to inflict on one's carpool companions
a past address. LOOK AT ME, NOT MAKING
IT ABOUT ME. But what would anyone
have to say, except OH? They never
were there. They don't know the insolent
kitchen. They can't still smell the skewers
in the foil tin, or the stink of shots
at a late hour, when guests had mostly gone.
That must have been J's fortieth.
Or maybe the vigil for T? This is why
we shouldn't have occasions. Same crowd,
same food, same room—it runs together.
A scene in my mind seems buoyant, and then
I realize. But even worse is the other
way around. Why is it that any time I half-
ascend this heap of pain, I get cut down?

Good Share

An airport—like a hog farm,
like a landfill, like a graveyard—

has to go somewhere. An airport
has to go somewhere, so
why not here? I nominate you

and you and me to roil
in our respective beds while planes

fly so low overhead we can tell
what makes they are. The yowl
of the Airbus, the Boeing's

Gregorian roar. At least they drown
out the rest of this inexcusably human

night: longneck bottle greeting
the side of a passing car,
strange chanting, fistfight too close

to the tracks, the neighbors
with their nonstop innovation

in the arena of sex-offender-registry
drinking games. View the mug shot,
guess the offense, drink a shot if

you're wrong. Eleven men in ten
locations: guess which two guys

split a duplex. Drink a shot
if you're wrong. Plug in the ocean
in order to find out if anyone's

currently in the ocean and if
we, consequently, should avoid it.

Do you think we should avoid it?
Drink a shot if you're
wrong. Drink while you can,

because I heard from a dead guy
there's no alcohol in Heaven.

I also heard no alcohol
on Earth. If you're drinking right
now, buddy, you're in Hell.

It Used to Be We Had to Go to War

just to make enough dead men
to give up to God. Then God stopped
caring for sacrifice, but you know
how it is with old habits. The scientist,
hauled to the Capitol to justify
his new particle lab, finally spit out
CONGRESSMAN, IT HAS NOTHING
TO DO WITH DEFENDING
OUR COUNTRY, EXCEPT TO MAKE
OUR COUNTRY WORTH DEFENDING.
Yes, it is our duty, here on the home
front, to ensure there is always
a new thing to kill and die for.
A heartier engine, a stickier resin,
a toothier starlet, a stonier statue,
a seamier alley in which you and I
might meet. A livelier, more festive
substitute for party balloons. Consider
ditching the Mylar and replacing
with paper bunting, replacing with
ivy or drumming or the smell
of something burning. Consider
replacing with high-end
angular haircuts. Consider replacing
with invitees being waited on
by serfs. Consider replacing with
colorful yet orderly mass
suicide—just make it enough
of a regular thing, and the children
won't know what they've missed.

During the Strife, My Sisters

began to stage an old play
about how women, by holding back sex,
could force the armistice

THE ONLY WEAPON WE HAVE—

and others of my sisters,
infuriated, stormed the stage in protest

singing how can you announce this is all
we are
            receptacles

when women are out there mapping
the marshland, scrambling
the phone lines, bombs in our pockets,
rushing the roadblock

THE ONLY WEAPON WE HAVE—

sisters, can't we meet here in the middle
fuck them all, bear their sons

then spirit the babies into the woods,
leave them to waste in the bramble

and then we walk away spitting and grinding

our boots in the mud and tracking
it everywhere

And Also with You

The comet taught us how to watch the war.
The comet contended that fire

is romantic and recommended we each behold it alone,
envisioning out there somewhere our next
lover, craning up at this same sky.

Was the comet simply endeavoring
to keep us divided, we asked it, and the comet

did not reply. Then we discovered the men
who wanted us dead
were convening at night on the site where their hero

had been unceremoniously
interred. And so we exhumed the guy, burned him up,
and fed his ash to the rapids,

to be churned into marlstone and mud-rich
air. Good thinking. Now he's everywhere.

Good Description

Lord I am such a narcissist—I couldn't
even give a good
description, having been thinking only
of myself and what
in my body was breaking and how unmendable
the break, thinking only of
myself and with what archaic charge
was I complying, crying over and over NO,
as though to reduce confusion
as to whether I'd given permission,
when nobody, for that, would give
permission—I mean only
a true narcissist would expect to be faithfully
obeyed, and Lord I
am such a narcissist—I think I am so
charming, so kittenish and cultured,
uproarious at parties,
enlivening conversations with my extensive
knowledge of strangling,
how pressure around a person's neck
will cause a contact lens to dislodge from the iris,
making it hard to see, but that's not funny,
not funny to anyone
except the company that slices
and sells the lenses—they never turn down
a chance to sell replacements,
so at least somebody's
smiling, cozying up with a cup of cream
of potato, flipping on the money
channel, watching that arrow soar—

The Beach

In theory I don't
like it but then when I'm there

I remember how in so many
other locations
it is not considered permissible
behavior to splay facedown
and speak to no one

the beach

is one of the few spots left
where you get spared
where you may excuse yourself
from the performance of
these clabbered conversations

one person explaining the fortune
teller on Highland Avenue
couldn't make rent and hammered
the storefront shut

the other spouting back SHOULDN'T
SHE HAVE PREDICTED, BEING
A FORTUNE TELLER AND ALL, THAT WAS
GOING TO HAPPEN

sour pattern

anyway that's not what they do
it's not like she's in there informing
people which semiconductor
stock is fixing to split or in what
year they'll get divorced

it's more silhouetted
it's not like she's in there

cautioning walk
with another person that night

keys will be hardly, the fortune
reader isn't in there screaming,
weapon enough

the beach

the terns and the metal detectors
the sensation of combing
through sediment witlessly

another person
would not have been knocked

into the air and propelled
toward the copious bramble
would not have stayed there all night
would not have required returning
the next day
in hopes of retrieval

kneeling
scrutinizing the thistle

Don't Spend It All in One Place

The whole thing about museums is they don't
let you have a pen; it is formally prohibited to write
with a pen while proximate to the collection.
The only appropriate response is scorn—just what
do they think is going to happen? Do they envision me
slipping, flailing with pen-hand extended,
and somehow streaking ink all over their corrugated
sculpture of a big tin knot? Mocking the prospect
of a museumgoer scarring the art helps me forget
about all the times it has of course happened:
acid splatter across the Dutch nude, hammer to the arm
of the PIETÀ. Or the pipe bomb placed beside
the high relief. Or the man who drew his gun
and shot up a wall of old masters and then himself.

Attacks on artwork are common enough, but it's not
as though every odd watercolor gets its own
day to be maimed. It's more that specific paintings
enter into cycles of finding themselves slashed
and restored, punched through and restored, effaced
by aerosol and then restored. Once a painting
gets famous for having absorbed some disturbance,
everyone wants to have a go. It's like the woods
where a few people killed themselves and then all
of a sudden all these tourists were planning
pilgrimages there to do the same. The woods
were in an area accessible only by ferry, and after
a while the agency that governed the ferry system
declared it a crime to purchase a one-way ticket.

What I want to know is what does it mean to take out
anger on an object—can pummeling something
that won't experience knowledge of its own breaking
be productive, or does it simply commonize
misdirected violence? Make it okay. I gave my dog
a human name, and sometimes when I encounter
people who share that name, I mention it and watch
them appear affronted, as though I'm somehow calling
them a dog. Should I have chosen instead the name
of a painting, as a painting would just take it—is that
what they're made for? Like the new-to-market
robot that's ostensibly for cleaning, but everyone knows
its primary function is dipping its optimized
head in a show of deference. Can't keep it in stock.

The magnate hyping his new memoir of depression,
in interviews across a range of platforms, repeats
and repeats the line that he knew he was ill
when he surveyed the unchecked magnitude of his
holdings and still felt numb. What I want to know is
not the sum, but the specific assets that dared
deliver no thrill. There must have been art.
Everyone wonders what happens to stolen paintings,
and it's common to speculate that they end up
hoarded in the climatized chambers of stealth
collectors. Is that what they're made for? To marshal
their beauty in the service of diagnosis? In that case,
nobody needs them. We already have that power,
to stare back at tycoons and have them feel nothing.

For what I was made, no one has said, but my own
arc doesn't seem to be the answer. I'm not put out,
having been instructed it is an honor to exist on
this earth for the story of somebody else.
To emblematize their wishes and dreads, to model
and mollify. Look at songbirds, how they're only
around so our dead might appear to us as them
and thereby avoid the shame of recurring as objects.
Or the ninety-year-old sea turtle in the aquarium's
briny dim, who allows onlookers to pride themselves
on not yet having grown old, on being comparatively
lithe and hot. This wish to feel young—recalling
my own past, I can't imagine desiring to go backward,
but of course I am aware it's a popular longing.

The predominant response to acts of outcry—
whether directed against a museum or merely
executed within its walls—is to archive the evidence,
wait fifty years, and then mount a broadly publicized
retrospective: FIFTY YEARS OF PROTEST ART.
Any other approach is plainly wasteful—eat up
what's put before you, or step aside. We're in
lean times. It's like with my neighbor, every morning
scavenging the news—she recently started dating
a guy from a region now under invasion, and she
plans their conversations. I see her getting gooey
at the mention of a fresh blockade or gassing, excited
for the two of them to drink and decry it that evening.
Days when the war is dormant, she's almost grieving.

A therapist once assured me he had enough money
to purchase outright a late-model luxury
car, but he drove something unremarkable instead.
His whole thing was he didn't want his patients,
walking past his parking space, to nurture
resentments, to conceptualize their pain as a kind
of fuel for his modish life. That never made
sense—wouldn't he want the costliest car on offer,
so his patients could see it plainly and be assured
they understood where their dollars were going?
They know he has money. Now they'll go wild
imagining him spending on things unseen, parking
his dump of a car outside of the men's boutique,
striding in and petting a stack of silk briefs.

THEY SPENT MORE ON THE OUTSIDE THAN ON
THE INSIDE, I overheard someone say in the ticket line
to enter a redone museum, to which her friend
responded LOOK WHO'S TALKING. They were both
wearing black and their clothing matched
the matte of the curved facade. It was like that joke
you're supposed to make when someone shows up
wearing military camouflage print for personal style:
I ALMOST DIDN'T SEE YOU! I prefer a different
bit, in which I imagine that everyone sporting
woodland-pattern anoraks and desert-pattern pumps
is enlisted in a single stateless army, and I feel my
own fear of them and my propulsion to hand over
whatever they want, but what do they want?

FIFTY YEARS OF PROTEST ART. Somewhere between
the cast-polymer dynamite at the palace door
and the offset lithograph WE WON'T FIGHT
ANOTHER RICH MAN'S WAR, a museum might also
want to present a show of its own obstructions—
you're nothing in this town if you can't
monetize your sins. Combing through the archives,
they'll hit on a trove of letters from eminent
artists, sent in protest when the museum started,
lamenting the ticket price of fifty cents. That
was big money then. SHOULD ACCESS TO ART BE
RESTRICTED TO PEOPLE OF MEANS? Frame it,
tack it to the wall. The cost of a ticket today is twenty
dollars, an increase of thirty-nine hundred percent.

Some museums get famous for having been robbed—
institutions with this distinction can include with their
twenty-dollar ticket an exhibit of the empty frames.
SHOULD ABSENCE OF ART BE RESTRICTED
TO PEOPLE OF MEANS? When the policy states that
carryalls must be left at the lobby desk, I always
wonder if their worry isn't weapons, but empty
space—is it formally prohibited to walk the length
of the gallery floor with a hollow in your bag precisely
the dimensions of Rembrandt's only seascape?
Mocking the bag-check protocol helps me forget
about the tavern scene with the bullet holes right
through it, how it continued to be shown and did
its display of damage make it more valuable or less.

Give them what they want. But what do they want?
Ultimately, I find this place to be a fully predatory
city. Electric fences, post-op sepsis, the insult
NO ONE EVER SAW HER FIRST. You can't even stand
and wait for your train without someone suffering
from an acute case of undercongratulation
praying for you to shuffle to the edge of the platform
and teeter over, so that he might intervene and be seen
as a savior. Moving through an intersection
the other day, I passed a young child who was deep
in a screaming fit: NO NO NO NO, and I suddenly
suspected the child was me—the child I used to be,
transported somehow ahead and horrified
to find what the future brings. She did have my eyes.

Really, though, I'm losing track of time. In the film
depicting a bygone war, everything feels
like the future, even the scene where a luminous
woman appears in a doorframe and all the troops
goggle and shove: OUT OF MY WAY—OUT OF MY WAY—
I SAW HER FIRST. People are so preoccupied
with looks. I remember how the tract against suicide
posited exposure to art and plants as antidote
to despair, making the argument that beauty will buoy
the hopeless. What a jab at the scarlet moss
and slender pine of the woods, at hundreds of years
of portraiture and plein air. I take it they just weren't
pretty enough to convince anyone to abandon
their plans. I take it NO ONE EVER SAW THEM FIRST.

Spotting a man in a flat wool cap with lines at his eyes
and mouth, I thought, that's how my friend D
will look in ten years. Then I realized—no, that's what
he looks like now. I am losing track of time. I can't
even view a painting anymore without picturing
its future: knife-marks, singes, punctures in the canvas,
patches of varnish half-eaten by splatters of lye.
Of course that's hardly the full extent of the methods—
I've been meaning to learn them all, but I'm afraid
to read any further on the subject, even though I know
it's childish to fear reading. It's like being scared
by a movie, needing water but hesitating to enter
the kitchen, having hours earlier watched someone
get it in a gray room, awl through the neck—

Ultimately, it's a mystery why anyone would choose
to visit a museum, to accumulate more and more
images they'll only end up begging to forget.
I can't even go near a painting anymore without
wondering at what point will it finally get encased
in protective glass—this won't stop anyone
from hurling objects in its direction, but it will
result in the shattering of most projectiles.
And the painting just hanging there afterward,
surrounded by smashed fruit and splintered
pottery, like some disfavored leader—I can't not
see it. I can't not think of the queue in the marbled
entry hall, the counter, the request for a one-way
ticket to the gallery. That'll be ten bucks.

Other Things, If Not More Urgent Things

How to get close without going over.
How to feign lust for whatever's on offer.
How the largest possible quantity
of anything is a lifetime. A lifetime
of oat bran. A lifetime of timing belts.
A lifetime of saying SURE, WHY NOT,
I'M ONLY ON EARTH X NUMBER
OF YEARS, and not knowing what
to make x. Sometimes I pick a number
I've already passed. I remember
the gambler's credo—when you only
have fifty bucks left in this world,
you'd better get rid of it fast; the last
thing you want is money around,
reminding you every day of the money
you lost. The recommended
retirement plan is arabesque, then leap
and smash on the seawall. We made
a promise not to catch each other.

Some Toxin

This is what we get. This is the penance
for extending and extending the human lifespan—
now some people live a hundred and twenty years,
but those years are increasingly spent being bombarded
with adorable profiles of the oldest people,
interviews about what keeps them ticking.
The secret is always some toxin, like bacon or vodka,
and the joke that ensues is always the same:
THE CHEMICALS PRESERVE HIM. That's all fine,

but just once I would like to uncrumple the Metro section
and find that the key to long life is rage and trauma,
that bitterness girds the organs in equal measure.
If I could choose to be born in any era,
I would opt to predate these longer lives.
There's so much violence, always. Better to have it
visited on you back when your attackers
would end up dead much sooner. When you would die
sooner, too. All I want is for someone

to understand me, but it seems my keenest friends
and I—we've scattered. We've struggled for peace,
for permanence, and somehow in that struggle,
we've ventured far from each other. This is what
we get. This is the penance. Back when even the powerful
died younger, they would lose one another and dutifully
wait to be reunited in Heaven. We wait for that
still, but now in the absence of Heaven. We say someday
we'll find each other, year after year on Earth.

Fake Sick

The past is the same as anything else—we built it
and now we can't kill it. We keep lurching

at it with the scoring ax and connecting
with the walls instead. That punishing season—

the hall light's hiss, the door off its hinge—

I'm ready to stop remembering. The trouble is
there's nobody else who can do it. A memory

isn't a metal grille drawn down on a storefront
at night, then unlocked in the morning.
You can't fake sick, call in. There's no other person

to wake in the slate dawn, drive into downtown,
locate the recess, collapse the gate, maneuver

the thing out of view. There's only you.

Home, Followed by Tall Buildings

Why do I have to remember the whole
of the trauma, can't we

split it—

You take the unburnt brick eye of the well
I'll take the list of top spots for suicide, ranked

Remember after the funeral
the teenagers played charades

GODFATHER II—

First syllable: niece in her velvet
blazer, down on her knees and praying

Then waving her palms around her
in all directions

I knew it was GOD—

I knew it by how, like God, she pretended
to reach everywhere, but she didn't

And Stay Out

Rough days I'm trying to live
as though dead, to satisfy
or at least dampen the inclination
to actually die. I'm holding
mainly still. I'm forming my face
into no specific expression.
I'm lowering the lights
so I can't see my poster
of one world leader grinning
and shattering, over the head
of another, a trick bottle
of champagne—a dead person
wouldn't be looking at that,
or at anything. Stop thinking
about the theory that slaughter
has coarsened the population,
that the only ones who
managed to stay hale or half-well
in atrocious times were the ones
who wouldn't share,
who would tear from smaller
arms damp rations and standard-
issue disaster blankets—part
wool, part synthetic, resistant
to flame. Stop knowing that these
were the only people who lived
long enough to pass
themselves on. To breed.
Stop being absurd. And stop
saying breed. Dead
people don't need that word.

Ohio on TV

Crucifixes on layaway. Absence of dead bolts.
Deep-fried sucralose.

Whole families living out of abandoned pianos.

Sometimes in cerebral hour-long dramas,
the characters must go to Ohio,
and this is the way it looks. How do they not know

it's the same here as anywhere else:
the poverty is mundane, the wealth outrageous?

And no one is nice.

I myself return here only to party
with people who pummel me, to follow
them around like a patchy

dog in a TV scene that takes place
in Ohio. We walk by the oblong enclosure
where the city is staging its summer fling.

You can drink a bourbon out of a pineapple rind.

I think it's intended to make you feel
like you are a part of something, connected back
by the long straw in your mouth.

I'm desperate to travel in time

to before we all started treating each other
so poorly, but I know I would be like the character

whose power is she can wind back the clock,
but only for three minutes.
It's not long enough to prevent anything.

It's only enough time to tear through the downtown
bawling and then watch it all happen again.

Fifty

He said IF YOU KEEP PUNISHING
YOURSELF LIKE THIS YOU'LL BE OLD

BY THE TIME YOU'RE FIFTY
and right there in the instant
of him saying it I became fifty

I was never able to go back

and it was never made clear to me
what might have transpired
in the obliterated years between

had I performed myself inside them
exceedingly quickly or had I

not lived them at all

I felt as though I had memories
a deaccessioned painting
a hovel with keyhole doorway

anecdotes of conglomerates
and their cocktail-napkin origins

was I supposed to be charmed

hardest of all was the recentness
of every egregious outburst

every midnight plummet
the adjacency I couldn't wish away
I was fifty and my worst

mistakes I'd made just yesterday

Pennsylvania

Other children, when I was a child,
would at times invoke the inner light—

I misunderstood.

I thought it meant God scorches
within us, and God, like a torch,

can go out. That was so long ago.
I've since ceased my believing in death—

there's no such thing.

There's only a kind of brownout,
the whole of the globe turning

off for a moment, then shuddering
back, the same as it was,

except one person short.

And then before long, an utter new
person is born. Somebody worse.

Acknowledgments

Many thanks to the editors of the publications in which poems from this book first appeared, sometimes in alternate versions: *The Adroit Journal, AGNI, The American Poetry Review, The Arkansas International, The Awl, The Believer, Bennington Review, Brick, Granta, Gulf Coast, The Hampden-Sydney Poetry Review, The Hong Kong Review, Kenyon Review, The Los Angeles Review of Books, Memorious, Mississippi Review, Narrative, The New Yorker, The New York Review of Books, Poetry, Poetry London, Provincetown Arts, Sidereal Magazine, Southeast Review, Subtropics,* and *Washington Square Review.*

I am grateful to the Center for the Humanities at Tufts, the Griffin Trust for Excellence in Poetry, the Massachusetts Cultural Council, and the Somerville Arts Council. Many thanks, also, to Becky Alexander, Will Barron, Erin Belieu, Jamie Boyle, Adam Clay, Rebecca Morgan Frank, Kathy Fagan Grandinetti, Ann Hamilton, Matt Hooley, Lisa Lowe, David Lynn, Mike Maday, Susan Maday, Tyler Meier, Elizabeth Lindsey Rogers, Cormac Slevin, Pablo Tanguay, Craig Morgan Teicher, and Jillian Weise. I am grateful for my inspiring colleagues and students at Tufts, and for all the support I have found there. Thank you to everyone at *KR.* Thank you to Michael Wiegers and to all the ingenious people at Copper Canyon Press. Thanks to all my parents, my sister, my in-laws, and my siblings-in-law. And to Martha. And one thousand times to the knockout R and to the shining F.

Lannan Literary Selections

For two decades Lannan Foundation has supported the publication and distribution of exceptional literary works. Copper Canyon Press gratefully acknowledges their support.

LANNAN LITERARY SELECTIONS 2020

Mark Bibbins, *13th Balloon*

Victoria Chang, *Obit*

Leila Chatti, *Deluge*

Philip Metres, *Shrapnel Maps*

Natalie Shapero, *Popular Longing*

RECENT LANNAN LITERARY SELECTIONS FROM COPPER CANYON PRESS

Sherwin Bitsui, *Dissolve*

Jericho Brown, *The Tradition*

John Freeman, *Maps*

Jenny George, *The Dream of Reason*

Ha Jin, *A Distant Center*

Deborah Landau, *Soft Targets*

Maurice Manning, *One Man's Dark*

Rachel McKibbens, *blud*

Aimee Nezhukumatathil, *Oceanic*

Camille Rankine, *Incorrect Merciful Impulses*

Paisley Rekdal, *Nightingale*

Natalie Scenters-Zapico, *Lima :: Limón*

Frank Stanford, *What About This: Collected Poems of Frank Stanford*

Ocean Vuong, *Night Sky with Exit Wounds*

C.D. Wright, *Casting Deep Shade*

Javier Zamora, *Unaccompanied*

Matthew Zapruder, *Father's Day*

Ghassan Zaqtan (translated by Fady Joudah), *The Silence That Remains*

About the Author

Natalie Shapero is the author of two previous collections, *Hard Child* and *No Object*, and her writing has appeared in *The New York Times Magazine*, *The New Yorker*, *Poetry*, and elsewhere. She teaches at Tufts University.

Poetry is vital to language and living. Since 1972, Copper Canyon Press has published extraordinary poetry from around the world to engage the imaginations and intellects of readers, writers, booksellers, librarians, teachers, students, and donors.

WE ARE GRATEFUL FOR THE MAJOR SUPPORT PROVIDED BY:

THE PAUL G. ALLEN
FAMILY FOUNDATION

CULTURE

Lannan

TO LEARN MORE ABOUT UNDERWRITING
COPPER CANYON PRESS TITLES,
PLEASE CALL 360-385-4925 EXT. 103

WE ARE GRATEFUL FOR THE MAJOR SUPPORT PROVIDED BY:

Anonymous

Jill Baker and Jeffrey Bishop

Anne and Geoffrey Barker

In honor of Ida Bauer, Betsy
Gifford, and Beverly Sachar

Donna and Matthew Bellew

Will Blythe

John Branch

Diana Broze

John R. Cahill

The Beatrice R. and Joseph A.
Coleman Foundation

The Currie Family Fund

Laurie and Oskar Eustis

Austin Evans

Saramel Evans

Mimi Gardner Gates

Gull Industries Inc. on behalf of
William True

The Trust of Warren A. Gummow

Carolyn and Robert Hedin

Bruce Kahn

Phil Kovacevich and Eric Wechsler

Lakeside Industries Inc. on behalf
of Jeanne Marie Lee

Maureen Lee and Mark Busto

Peter Lewis and Johnna Turiano

Ellie Mathews and Carl Youngmann
as The North Press

Hank and Liesel Meijer

Jack Nicholson

Gregg Orr

Petunia Charitable Fund and
adviser Elizabeth Hebert

Gay Phinny

Suzanne Rapp and Mark Hamilton

Adam and Lynn Rauch

Emily and Dan Raymond

Jill and Bill Ruckelshaus

Cynthia Sears

Kim and Jeff Seely

Joan F. Woods

Barbara and Charles Wright

Caleb Young as C. Young Creative

The dedicated interns and
faithful volunteers of
Copper Canyon Press

The Chinese character for poetry is made up of two parts:
"word" and "temple." It also serves as pressmark for
Copper Canyon Press.

The poems are set in Sabon.
Book design and composition by Phil Kovacevich.

CPSIA information can be obtained
at www.ICGtesting.com
Printed in the USA
JSHW020948060223
37299JS00003B/5

9 781556 595882